FESTIVALS! USA

A Midwestern Corn Festival
Ears Everywhere

Lisa Gabbert

The Rosen Publishing Group's
PowerKids Press™
New York

To Sandra, who finds magic in the ordinary.

Published in 1999 by The Rosen Publishing Group, Inc.
29 East 21st Street, New York, NY 10010

First Edition

Book Design: Michael de Guzman

Photo Credits: p. 4 © Michael Von Ruber/International Stock; p. 7 © Jack Zehrt/FPG International; p. 8 © Bob Firth/International Stock; p. 11 © Michael Goldman/FPG International; p. 12 © Ron Maratea/International Stock; pp. 15, 16, 19, 20 © Joe Viesti/Viesti Associates, Inc.

Gabbert, Lisa.
    A midwestern corn festival: ears everywhere/ by Lisa Gabbert.
        p.   cm. — (Festivals! USA)
    Includes index.
    Summary: Explains the importance of corn as a crop and examines the rides, pageants, and other activities at a corn festival.
    ISBN 0-8239-5341-6
    1. Harvest festivals—Middle West—Juvenile literature. 2. Corn—Juvenile literature.
    [1. Harvest festivals. 2. Corn. Festivals.] I. Title. II. Series.
GT4407.G33 1998
394.26—dc21
                                                     98-15543
                                                       CIP
                                                       AC

Manufactured in the United States of America

Contents

Corn as a Crop

Corn is a grain. It belongs to the same family as wheat, rye, rice, oats, and barley. Along with these grains, corn is used to make bread, tortillas, and cereal. Many people like corn in its natural form—right off the cob!

At one time, corn grew in the wild. Today, it is a **domesticated** (doh-MES-tih-kay-ted) plant. This means that corn cannot shed its seeds without a farmer's help. Corn is an important crop in the United States.

In the past, farmers had to pick corn with their hands. Today, big machines do this work for them.

The Corn Belt

The corn belt is an area of the United States where the most corn is grown. This area is also part of the Midwest, and includes the states of Illinois, Indiana, Iowa, Minnesota, Missouri, and Nebraska.

There are many different kinds of corn. Blue corn gets its name from its color. Sweet corn has a lot of natural sugar, so it tastes sweet. Dent corn has a small dent in each kernel. Ninety percent of all corn grown in the United States is dent corn.

Many cornfields can be found in the Midwest, such as this one in Illinois.

Using Corn

Corn is used in many different ways. It is eaten as corn on the cob, popcorn, tortillas, corn bread, and cornflakes. But did you know that ketchup, ice cream, sausage, and margarine all have corn as an **ingredient** (in-GREE-dee-ent)? That's because many foods contain corn syrup, which is used as sugar, or corn oil, which is used in cooking. But foods are not the only things made from corn. Batteries, plastics, papers, and cosmetics sometimes use products made from corn.

◀ *You have probably eaten corn in one form or another. How about popcorn at the movies?*

Maize

Europeans who came to the Americas had never seen corn until Native Americans showed it to them. Native Americans have been using corn, or **maize** (MAYZ), for about 8,000 years. At first, it was grown from a grass called **teosinte** (tay-oh-SIN-tay). Mexican farmers were the first to grow maize, but as time passed, maize spread as far as South America. It became the main food for most native **civilizations** (sih-vih-lih-ZAY-shunz), including the Aztec, Incan, and Mayan.

The cornfields of native civilizations probably looked much like this present-day cornfield in Guatemala. ▶

Harvest Festivals

A corn festival is a **harvest** (HAR-vest) festival. Harvest festivals celebrate a good crop. Like other harvest festivals, corn festivals usually happen in the late summer or fall.

Today, corn festivals are called different names, such as Corn Fest, Popcorn Days, Corn Carnival, Sweet Corn Festival, and Corn on the Cob Day. But they all have the same purpose—to celebrate corn.

◄ *If there is a lot of corn at harvesttime, farmers know a corn festival will soon follow!*

Corn Festival and Fair Activities

Many corn festivals are like state or county fairs. Often there is an agricultural show for corn and other vegetables such as squash, tomatoes, and pumpkins. There are also **livestock** (LYV-stok) and flower shows. Many corn festivals have carnival rides and games. There are pony rides, petting zoos, music and dancing, and flea markets too. Sometimes people make crafts that use corn, such as corn-husk dolls, brooms, and mats.

Sometimes corn festivals even have games that involve corn, such as corn-shucking contests. ▷

Corn-Eating and Other Contests

Eating corn is a big part of a corn festival. And **competitions** (kom-peh-TIH-shunz) are an important part of midwestern corn festivals. A corn-eating competition is a contest to see who can eat the most pieces of corn on the cob. There are also pie-eating contests, turtle races, car races, and agricultural competitions. Prizes are given out for the biggest or best animals, vegetables, or homemade foods such as pies and jams.

Corn that you eat at a corn festival might be some of the sweetest and freshest corn you'll ever have.

17

Corn Queens

Almost every corn festival has a corn queen **pageant** (PA-jent). The crowning of the corn queen is a popular event. Usually, the girls in the competition have just graduated from high school. They are judged for their work in the **community** (kuh-MYOO-nih-tee). The winner receives a crown and a big bouquet of flowers. Sometimes she rides in the festival parade and receives a prize, such as money for college. The winner also gets her name and photograph printed in the local newspaper.

A corn queen is someone who can proudly represent her community. ▶

Corn and Community

Corn festivals are local events. This means they are only celebrated by people who live in the same town or city. Sometimes corn festivals are hosted by special groups that want to raise money for a **charity** (CHA-rih-tee).

Having a festival is one way that people show they belong to and care about their community.

Many members of a community like to help out during their harvest or at corn festivals.

Green Corn Festivals

Some Native Americans also hold important corn festivals. One of them is called the Native American Green Corn Festival. This festival celebrates the first green growth of the small corn plant or the first ripening of the corn's ears. This festival also celebrates Native American **heritage** (HEH-rih-tij), the importance of corn as a Native American food, and the importance of being Native American.

There may be a corn festival happening near you!

Broom Corn Festival	Arcloa, IL
Lenni Lenape Roasting Ears of Corn Festival	Allentown, PA

Glossary

charity (CHA-rih-tee) An organization that helps a specific group that's in need.

civilization (sih-vih-lih-ZAY-shun) A group of people living in an organized and similar way.

community (kuh-MYOO-nih-tee) A group of people who live near each other and have something in common.

competition (kom-peh-TIH-shun) A contest.

domesticated (doh-MES-tih-kay-ted) To be living in a tame environment; not wild.

harvest (HAR-vest) A season's gathered crop.

heritage (HEH-rih-tij) The cultural traditions that are handed down from parent to child.

ingredient (in-GREE-dee-ent) An item needed to make something else.

livestock (LYV-stok) Farm animals.

maize (MAYZ) The Native American word for corn.

pageant (PA-jent) A group of people celebrating together, as in a parade.

teosinte (tay-oh-SIN-tay) The grass from which corn developed.

Index